Paws for Thought
Life through a dog's eyes

Paws for Thought

Life through a dog's eyes

ELAINE JACQUES

Text Elaine Jacques
Copyright © Elaine Jacques

First print February 2024
ISBN: 9978-1-917129-22-0
Hb

Welcome to a doorway into the life of a border collie called Monty. Where you will experience the wonders of his life in his own words. This book is dedicated to all our furry friends and the humans, who share in the joy our furry companions so selflessly give us, each and every day. To children and adults alike who have yet to embark on the wonderful journey that their future companions will bring. I celebrate you all, but above all I dedicate these pages to my Monty who single handily saved me from myself. What does Monty mean to me? In a word, everything. He is my home, my muse, my inspiration and my reason. This book is testament to what a remarkable dog Monty is.

CONTENTS

CHAPTER 1 2014	11
CHAPTER 2 LADY	15
CHAPTER 3 SCHOOL DAYS	21
CHAPTER 4 MY PAD	27
CHAPTER 5 - BABY RESCUE	29
CHAPTER 6 DOGGY PADDLING	33
CHAPTER 7 GRANDAD DEL	39
CHAPTER 8 NAN	43
CHAPTER 9 OOPSIE I DID A WHOOPSIE	47
CHAPTER 10 THE GREAT ROAD TRIP	53
CHAPTER 11 ISLAND LIFE	59
CHAPTER 12 HAPPY WOOF WOOF TO ME	67
CHAPTER 13 A DOG IS NOT JUST FOR	71

CHRISTMAS

CHAPTER 14 FOR THE LOVE OF WOODS   75
& SQUIRRELS

CHAPTER 15 GOING VEGGIE   81

CHAPTER 16 WHAT THEY SAY   87

CHAPTER 1 2014

2014 was a distressing year. Without warning, my purpose in life was ripped out of me. I was told I would never be a mother in the most conventional way. Something I had not only always wanted, but never suspected that I never would. The mental pain was soul-destroying, the physical pain from numerous surgeries unbearable. I was empty, lost, incredibly sad and my confidence had hit rock bottom. Everything that made me a woman, had been taken out from me. I felt desperately lonely and empty and it was at this time that I entertained the thought of getting a dog.

I had a lot of time on my hands, at home recovering from yet more surgery, and started scrolling and looking online for a pup. To be honest, I was heavily medicated at the time, so I can't remember too much.

But there must have been something about the ad for a collie pup that caught my eye. It was a small advert. Nothing flash.

'Border Collie puppies ready for a new home soon'

This could be a new start for the both of us. I wasn't allowed to drive, and it took some persuading to get my then husband to drive me out to the farm, where the pups were living. I suppose he thought I was reacting to my current situation and possibly not thinking of the long term responsibility? He was probably right but eventually he agreed.

It took us about half an hour to reach the farm. Not the most comfortable journey, but I definitely felt an air of excitement. When we arrived, we were greeted by a lovely couple, who had not long had a child themselves. That was a little hard, as I was still so raw. I suppose there would be reminders everywhere I went. We parked up and walked across the farm yard; being farm dogs, they lived outside in a pen. In total, there were 8 beautiful, obviously adorable bundles of puppiness. Some were black, some white and then one, who lived up to the tag of runt, a little odd, pigletty-looking puppy. His fur had not yet grown on his face which was pink with a matching whitish pinky nose and a black eye patch. He stood out. Seeing me, he straight away toddled over to me, and began trying to hug and climb my leg, 'pick me up, pick me up'. Looking down at him and his efforts there was an immediate connection. This puppy had chosen me! He wanted me. He would need me. I would need him. I felt an overwhelming sense of love and knelt down to pick him up.

My then-husband was adamant we should have one of the more 'perfect' looking puppies. I put my foot down, 'I'm paying, therefore I get to decide'.

The following six weeks were some of the longest in my life. I was so excited. I made sure to visit a few times, and took him a toy and a little blanket of mine, so he would get used to my smell. And I named him Monty. Each time I saw him, the connection grew stronger, until finally on a dark winter's night, I would not be driving home alone, nope, I would be sat on the back seat, with Monty on my lap. Hooray, Monty was coming home.

CHAPTER 2 LADY

I was born on a farm to amazing parents. My dad had a stunning white coat, and my mum wore her black coat with effortless elegance. Both my mum and dad had very important jobs chasing the sheep and things like that, they were masters at it. I noticed straight away I looked different to my brothers and sisters. They were much fluffier and I was definitely smaller than them. Maybe because I was the last one to pop out, my face was pink because I had no fur there yet. A little bit like a piglet.

Those early days were primarily spent nestling close to mum in the small outside house, I knew as home. Dad would go out for most of the day to work. It was that time of year when the sun shone a little less, and the leaves on the trees were changing from green to red and brown, the air was getting crisper, sometimes it would make my nose drip and if I walked around the house, the coolness would tickle my paws.

Being the little one, I would usually have to scramble my way over my brothers and sisters to squeeze in to get some of mum's warm milk. Although I couldn't see too well, I could smell the sweetness and I would follow my nose. At times the big people seeing me struggle would gently lift me and place me up to mum, ensuring I got my fair share. With a full, warm tummy, sleep would inevitably come quickly after. I cherished our naps together, strewn across or under one another a bit squashed, breathing through my little white button nose that was usually poking out from under one of the other furballs. It was cosy, safe and oh-so-comfy.

It wasn't very long before my eyes began to focus better. And I loved looking around taking in my surroundings. Tumbling around with my siblings. So much fun. We then started to have visitors. I got to know when they were coming, as I would hear a rumble in the courtyard, then one, two sometimes three and even four dull thuds, voices and a regular on-two-one-two clicking on the ground that grew louder and louder the closer it got. One particular day I heard those tell-tale sounds, so I sat up nice and straight. Oooooh another caller. We had certainly had a few lately. I enjoyed it even if I had no idea why they came. I stood up, looking forward to the attention I knew was on its way. They would make a fuss of us, tickle our tummies and make lots of noises. I loved it.

On this occasion, I watched as Lady came towards me. I can't quite put my paw on it, but I had a strong need to go sit on her lap and reassure her that everything would be ok. Call it doggy sixth sense. When she got close enough, I decided I would need to be bold and get noticed so, I padded over to her, showing off my little waggy tail, with my mission to get onto her lap. As I looked up it was clear this was not going to be as easy as I had thought it would be. It was much higher looking up from the bottom. No way I could jump, I would have to climb, after all, I had a lot of experience climbing over my brothers and sisters to get mum's milk. Should be a doddle. So, I grabbed her leg in a hug and began my attempt to shimmy up. It was a total failure as I just could not get a good grip. However, my valiant attempts must have done the trick, as when she looked down, I saw such kindness in her eyes, and she made herself smaller and gently helped me onto her lap. Her voice was so soothing, and I liked the strokes. I knew then, that whatever was going on here, this Lady would be a part of my world and future. And when she left to be honest, all I could think about was, when would I see her again.

Thank goodness I did and she did come back a few times. One day she even brought me a lovely soft blanket, it smelt so nice. And when she would leave, I would bury myself in it, and find comfort from that scent, and never stop wishing she would come back another time. Then on a dark and chilly night, she came again. I watched from the comfort of my blanket as her feet approached. She knelt down and scooped me up in the blanket, and pushed her nose into my fluffy neck, she smelt like my blanket. This time though she didn't put me back down. This time she carried me to the rumbling thing. The thing that brought her here. She climbed into the back, still cradling me. Then Man got in the front. Was this her house? It was quite different to mine. I was a little scared but also to be honest I felt a hint of excitement. And it was strange as I could still smell my brothers and sisters, even though they weren't there, but when I had a little snifferoo, I realised it was my old blanket from my bed right next to me. Suddenly a low rumble began, and I felt a funny vibration and we STARTED MOVING!!! What on earth?! Woaaah, this was a new experience and I liked it. I clambered up to peep back, and saw that my house got smaller and smaller. I was swaying side to side, then that stopped, I found my paws and felt more stable, less rocking about. I was so curious, what was happening? I managed to crawl up on Lady's shoulder to look out. WOW, it was dark, yet all I could see were white bright eyes chasing us. Sometimes they caught us but then would pass by us, and then I could just see red ahead. This was such a fun game and I was transfixed. I had never seen anything like it.

I'm not sure how much time elapsed but at some point, motion slowed and it felt like we were crawling forward a bit like how mum and dad did with the sheep. Then silence, the rumble stopped. Another cuddle from lady, thank you, and a rush of cold air passed over my little white nose. I felt a little uneasy when I was being carried through an opening, but Lady gave me a little additional hug, and I felt secure once more. Was I supposed to live here from now on? I reasoned then that I should pee at this place so that everyone would know it was my home. But where to go? There were strange shiny things on the floor, and I thought no way am I walking on them, and anyway where was the courtyard? Luckily lady had my back, and she carried me through the house to her outdoor space. It was different to my farm. Soft green stuff underfoot. But hey, it was outside and I needed to go.

Business done, at which point Lady made a lot of cooing noises (bit like the pigeons on the farm) and gave me another squeeze. I'm not sure what I did to be honest, but I must have done the right thing! Hooray.

Back inside I was able to take in my new surroundings. With both my blankets enveloping me, I could barely keep my eyes open, I felt so sleepy. Lady was next to me and she had a blanket too, I could just see her head poking out of it. So, I wriggled and curled into my blanket, still watching Lady. I thought, she seems nice. A new mum. I think I'm going to like it here. And suddenly just like that darkness flicked on. Silence. Sleep time.

My first night in my new home

CHAPTER 3 SCHOOL DAYS

I suppose first and foremost was piddle training. But straight away there was a problem. The shiny floor I previously mentioned. I have no idea what kind of floor it was but it scared the bejeevies out of me. And the problem was it was everywhere between me and the back door, which I would need to get to when I needed a wee. I'd never seen a surface like it. I did try and put a paw down, but instantly retracted it. It felt so alien. At this point I just sat on a mat and pretty much refused to cross that sea of glass. So, to begin with Mum would kindly pick me up and get me past it to get to the door.

It would take me absolutely ages to get over that floor fear. When I look back, I can't see why I was so frightened of it. But I was. Anyway, Mum had hung some bells on the back door. At first, I had no idea why. But she would take me across to the bells, lift my paw to them, tap them and they would make their tinkle sound. Then she would open the door and I would go for a wee. Maybe there was something in that, tinkle meant pee-pee? Well, that's what I thought, so after only about five times, of going through this process, when I next needed to go, I thought....I'm going to be brave and do this on my own, without mum guiding me. I went up by myself and gave a good pat on the bells. She came over and opened the door; and I rushed out to do my business, goodness what a relief! And mum went mad saying over and over what a good boy I was. Loads of hugs as well. I was well chuffed. When I was on the farm, I always went to the loo outside, so to me this was the natural thing to do. But my new Mum didn't need to know that!

I was definitely feeling more confident in my new home, and in those early months I confess I was a bit naughty. I blame it on teething. A bit painful that, but easily relieved with a bit of light chewing. I chewed everything. One time we were playing one of our favourite games, where one of us hides and the other has to find them. I was small enough to hide under the sofa, this was my most-liked hiding place. Mum would take forever to find me there because I had secretly chewed and gnawed my way through the base of the sofa, I could crawl under it and sit right up without being detected. I am a clever boy after all! I was and still am pretty decent at finding Mum, even when she plonks me in the middle of the room with a blanket over me. Off she creeps, to her hidey place. Then she calls me, and I charge from room to room to find her, sniffing around like mad. It never takes me long!

Oh, I remember, there was a time when my chewing was a bit out of control. I was wrestling with a sock; it had a good whiff too. So agreeable I ate it. It was very filling. Now I'm a regular dog, and found myself unable to do a poo. I tried and tried, to no avail. I think it was about two days later, when at last there was movement down that end. To my amazement, the sock started to come out. I might have got away with the embarrassment, but it got stuck, and I was literally waddling, around trying to shake it out. Frankly, it probably looked like I had another tail. Mum, saw my distress, and made the necessary emergency unpleasant decision to help the sock along, by taking it in her hands, where she proceeded to gently pull at it, encouraging me all the while to push. Mortifying really, but gradually I felt the pressure release and just like that I had birthed the sock. What a relief.

I was a good digger too. Mum had a fine-looking garden, so many plants, and nice turf to tear through. Such a hoot, furiously digging holes everywhere, foraging around and eating all the flora. It went a bit like this, I would burrow and mum would come along and fill the holes, so I would, of course, do it again, what a fun game, I think it was called 'no tut tut', because that's the kind of noise mum would make when I dug. I loved it!

I was born for learning, and home schooling was the best. I learnt to understand words, like my name to start with. When to sit down politely. And when Mum would throw a ball, to run after it and bring it back, because then she would throw it again. There was sweets training days too. Mum would line lots of different chewies up, and point at each one and say a word. She would do this over and over again, then she would stop pointing when she said the word. And I worked out she wanted me to show her the one she meant. So, I would give a nudge to the right one. And the best bit, when I got it right, which I soon did with ease, I would be allowed to eat it, a lovely treat. Growing up I was a quick learner, especially when treats were a-coming. I also learnt how to get dressed by myself. Mum would let me choose my collar for our daily walks. She would line them up so that I could have a good look at the selection, to be honest I would very much be guided by the season colours and what mum was wearing, it's nice to coordinate. I really liked being able to express my sense of fashion. I have great taste, don't you know.

Education was such fun, and I loved PE. Especially like dancing and hoop jumping. For a biggish dog I am surprisingly graceful at both. The dancing was fab, as Mum and I would dance like mad to 80's music. We must have looked a right pair!

Yeah, I was a brainy student. I did well and my schooling has served me well throughout my life.

Exploring the fawn and flora of my new garden

Garden digging!

CHAPTER 4 MY PAD

I must be one of the luckiest dogs on this planet. My bedroom is incredibly stylish, inviting and snug. When Mum is home, it's where I go to relax. Obviously, I don't sleep there at night, I sleep upstairs with Mum. But let me describe my room. My space is under the stairs. Mum took the door off the cupboard, to give it an open-plan feel. And it means I can see out all the time. I have a grey sofa in there with a fluffy blanket and behind me is a montage of photos of my friends and family, and my rosette I won in a beauty pageant. Yes, I know it's 4th, but hey it's a rosette. I also appreciate a bit of art so I have an oil painting that I'm very keen on. It's of a hound dog lying on a magnificent four poster bed. Probably some ancient King's dog. There is just something in the hound's eye that takes my breath away; it really is an impressive piece of art. Then I have my mood lighting jar. Inside are loads of green tennis balls, with fairy lights. It's very calming and gives a warm ambience and I feel very relaxed there.

My pad under the stairs

CHAPTER 5 - BABY RESCUE

I must tell you about the day I was a hero. I was only young and not had my first birthday. Mum's sister had come to visit with her new baby. I really love babies, but I do worry about them, I suppose they bring out the would-be parent in me. I feel a deep sense of protection. Well, the little thing was getting quite clever and could move about on all fours. Bit like a puppy. Even when they were chatting, I always kept a close eye on the baby. That day had been a washing day and Mum had loads of sheets to fold. Mum and her sister were upstairs with the baby. They were nattering away busily folding the sheets together, to put away in the airing cupboard when just for an instant they took their eye off the baby, who had by now crawled away to the edge of the stairs!

My heart thumped with fear and all I knew was I had to spring into action and prevent disaster. So, putting myself low to the ground on all fours, I strategically and very gently wriggled myself between the baby and the stair edge. It was quite risky, as neither did I want to tumble down. Then very delicately I began to nudge the baby away from the looming edge. Every time the baby would try to come back, I would nudge again. The naughty little baby probably thought it was a game. It felt like forever, but in all likelihood, it was probably only a few minutes. At which point Mum and her sister suddenly realised the baby was nowhere to be seen. They came very quickly out of the room and you can imagine their relief when they found baby! And they were so grateful and also astounded by my intuitive reaction, and that in effect I had saved the baby from what would have been a nasty roll down the stairs. It's just in my DNA to look after and protect my family.

Cuddles and a nap with Mum after busy hero work

CHAPTER 6 DOGGY PADDLING

One of the (many) awesome things with Mum, are the holidays and day trips we go on. I have literally been on trains, and when I'm not watching the landscape whizz past I like to read the paper and keep up to date with current affairs. Boat rides initially took a little getting used to, but I found my sea legs pretty quickly, and I do delight in the sea air blowing through my fur and watching the ships sailing by. I also love looking up to the skies watching all the birds. I have a natural sense of adventure and have visited and explored many interesting destinations, like the Isle of Wight, Brixham, Paington, Dartmouth and my favourites, Tintagel and Boss castle. I've even been rock climbing at Port Isaac cave, which in tales gone by was a smugglers cave, and you can only climb through when the tide is out. It's wet and slippery, and full of big rocks, I naturally just knew the way and put my best paw forward. Come on mum! This way, I barked and she followed. Others did too and they would say what a clever and brave boy I was. I must admit I was well proud when I reached the end and celebrated with a bark or two.

It was on one of our trips down to the coast by Watcombe Beach, that I learnt to swim. We were staying in a house with no stairs, and through the windows I could see lots of little boats. A breath-taking view across Brixham harbour and out to sea. D-Day came, we were down at the beach, and I was having a blast chasing birds, barking, running around, chasing my ball. The sea was lively, lots of little white foamy bits flicking off the top of the waves. When all of a sudden, Mum hitched her skirt up and stepped forward into the water. The waves rolling in over her feet. I'm Mum's bodyguard so it was clear I would have to follow. So, paws in.

The water was pretty cold and my paws sank a little in the sand, a strange sensation. I could see she had my ball, which she then chucked a little ahead. Well, all my friends know I can't resist a ball. I made my advance, trying to nimbly step over the waves, like a horse doing dressage, I got to the ball and brought it back. Then she threw it further. Now the fur under my belly was wet and swishing about, a bit like seaweed I had seen at the shoreline, I had never been this deep in my life. The ball was bobbing tantalisingly close. Again, I was able to retrieve it and take it back to Mum. By this point the waves were now properly catching me in the face, and when I licked my lips, I could taste salt. Mum then hurled the ball. By this time, I had gotten used to the water temperature and the mousiness of the waves, even getting the hang of jumping over them and therefore feeling more confident I dashed in. When all of a sudden, I felt weightless. I kid you not, I was bobbing, like my ball, which was by the way still some distance ahead. I was wildly trying to find some solid ground with my paws, waves spraying me loads, and fearing I was going to sink, I brought my paws up to my chin and started propelling them rapidly forward one after the other. Lo and behold, I found I was also moving closer towards the dipping ball. I made it to the ball and I successfully recovered it, turned around, yes, still paddling but harder with one leg, which enabled the turnaround manoeuvre, back to terra firma. Mum was waiting with loads of cuddles and kept saying over and over 'good boy Monty'. And that's how I learnt to swim. Today I love nothing better than swimming with Mum in the sea.

On the Train to London town, to see Big Ben. Lots of interesting smells there

Boating with mum in Brixham and feeling the sea air on my face

CHAPTER 7 GRANDAD DEL

I would like to tell you about the times I go to stay at my grandad Del's house. We have some comical moments like the occasion when he took me over to the fields. It was an exceptionally muddy day and he was doing what I love, throwing the ball for me. When I returned it after chasing it down, I saw he had gotten stuck in the mud right up to his knees. I sat with my head slightly tilted to the side as I usually do when tentatively watching with interest. There he was tugging at his feet trying to get out of the mud, and suddenly out came his left foot minus a shoe, which I found so funny! especially the next time when he put carrier bags on his feet. If the weather is really bad, say heavy rain he takes me to the back alley just behind the house so we don't get too wet. He throws the ball again and again. It's brilliant. I get a good run out there.

Oh yeah, there was another time when he took me to the local park one day. It was winter and it was snowing. When we crossed the road, he tripped over the curb which was hidden under the snow. He took a while to get up, and when he did, he was covered in the white stuff like a snowman but he was laughing at me because I was more worried about finding the ball (of course no ball would mean no park!).

Even when we are indoors, there is no let up for grandad Del. Hee hee. When he is watching TV, I put a toy on his foot. He ignores me. I sit there and stare at him, not blinking. He pretends not to notice and if the unwavering eye trick doesn't work, I go and get another toy and do the same again and again, he then eventually gives in.

I also know if I lick my lips long enough, he will give me some chicken. My powers of manipulation are next to none. We also have midnight feasts. When I'm at Mum's I like to go to bed early around 9pm. If she is still on the sofa watching the TV, I go and stand at the door and give her a reminder nod towards the stairs to say, 'come on, it's bedtime'. But at Dels's I've worked out he likes a bite to eat late at night before bed. So clever me has worked out that if I stay up, Del will share his snack with me. After I've had my snack I join mum upstairs in bed and leave grandad Del to rest.

Del has a greenhouse in his garden, and I enjoy keeping him company in there. He potters about and does things like feed the birds on the bird table. I help by making sure the smaller birds like sparrows, don't get bullied by the bigger greedier ones, like the pigeons which I chase away. I also make sure the birds are safe from roaming cats.

Grandad Del now has a mobility scooter that mum bought him as I suppose he is getting old (like me ha ha). And his legs get tired. But he still takes me out. He holds the lead and starts up the scooter. We start at a walking pace but he gradually speeds up and I find myself running alongside the mile into town. It's a good workout! On the occasional Sunday we go to his local club for a drink. I get to meet all his friends and I get a lot of attention.

Grandad Del is such a wag. I always have a great time at what I see as my second home.

Paws its cold!!

CHAPTER 8 NAN

I love my nan. Every time we go there, she gives me great big hugs and smothers me in kisses and always has presents for me. When she lived in the New Forest, we would go for fantastic long walks that she loved as much as me. Back then she didn't live too far from some beaches. I love beaches, the sea air, and running on the soft sand. Her nearest beach was Barton on Sea, about a 15-minute drive. The beach sits behind this huge cliff, though there are little paths from the village that will take you to the beach. Quite often nan would sit at the top, soaking in the sun while mum and I would nip down for a dip. Afterwards nan would treat us at the beach café, and she would order me some sausages. Perfect after a refreshing swim. There was one time when we all three of us went to Mudeford Beach (I still chuckle when I think about this). Mudeford is interesting. It's a sandbank and on one side it has lovely powdery white sand with little beach huts and then on the other side it's stony. On this particular day, mum and I were playing hide and seek (it's something we have always done since I was a pup). We were between the caravans and the beach. Mum then lobbed my ball over the wall, then swiftly leapt over it herself to go and hide. I was dying to go and chase it, but I waited until I heard Mum's whistle – my signal to spring into action. At which point I launched myself like a rocket over the wall, cleared the footpath, and narrowly missed some sunbathers. I was amazing. To be honest I surprised myself, and to this day it remains the biggest jump I ever accomplished. Nan and Mum were stunned at my athleticism and were in stitches. After that, we had a fab walk on the beach and then went to a café for drinks and snacks.

Another favourite place of mine we would go to was Highcliffe and its castle. From the village you can see needles pointing out of the sea. There is a very grand castle there too. What I relish about it are the ancient trees and sniffing their history. Lots of squirrels too, though I'm on the lead here so I can't give chase. When we would go there, I would get lots of attention from people, I'm a sociable creature so I lap it up. Then of course we would end up in the café. Yum.

Nan has moved now, and she lives in sheltered accommodation. She isn't as mobile as she used to be. We visit her regularly, and she has friends that go out to get me a prezzie for when I turn up. Since I have turned veggie, she has started giving me kale treats. They really are tasty. Mum probably thinks nan gives me too many treats. But nan is nan, and sometimes she pretends to Mum that a job needs doing, and then when Mum can't see she'll stealthily sneak me a biscuit. One time we were in the kitchen, she was sharing her crisps with me, I was very aware of the loud crunching they made, and trying to eat them as noiselessly as I could and obviously nan was being very quiet too so as not to attract Mum's attention, we thought we were being very smart. I then had a sense of being watched and yes, my senses were correct as, there was Mum standing in the doorway, we had been caught red-handed. Both nan and I stopped our crunching immediately, avoiding eye contact. But Mum wasn't angry, she thought it was comical and just smiled and wagged her finger at us both.

When we visit on a Sunday, we go out for roast dinners. They are the best. Nothing like walking into a carvery. The smells, gravy, chicken, veg. Literally, my stomach rumbles the minute we step in and I can't control my tail which moves like a fan set on the highest speed. Nan and Mum have their roasts at the table on plates and I have mine in a bowl next to them. If I think about it, if I miss anything since becoming a vegetarian it would be that. But I'm getting used to the roast with no chicken. As long as the veg are drowning in gravy I'm a happy boy.

I'm so lucky to have my nan, and when Mum says time to go and says goodbye, (yes, I understand the word!) I go to Nan and give her a big kiss. Then hop in the car homeward bound until the next time.

A great swim at Barton on Sea

CHAPTER 9 OOPSIE I DID A WHOOPSIE

I wasn't sure whether to share this 'experience' due to people's sensitivities, and if you are reading this over your breakfast, I highly advise you finish that first. This tale is not so much of an adventure, but more like possibly my most embarrassing moment thus far.

This was when we were living in West Sussex and Mum was working for Kew Gardens at Wakehurst. A magnificent wild botanic garden with acres and acres of land and weird and wonderful plants to smell and investigate. How do I know this? Well, I used to go to work with her, and when she was in the big house, she would take me for a run in the fields behind. I wasn't the only dog to go to work, there were a few others, including a couple of spaniels and a Jack Russell. I wouldn't say we were friends, more acquaintances at the office, I suppose colleagues. If we were walking on our leads in the massive grounds, our paws would cross, and we would slow down and have a friend's sniff.

Mum then changed office and moved from the big house to the Bothe. Our office was upstairs. It had that new smell, and was terrifically smart. There were a couple of other rooms too, where people went to work. On this day Mum seemed busier than usual, bustling about. As I suspected she had a very important visitor. A boss type. Instead of using the office to meet, she had set up at an open desk; by that I mean it wasn't exactly a room – just a desk in a space. A place where different people that I often didn't recognise would sit at and work. As was the norm, when Mum had a meeting, she would leave me to look after her office, another one of my responsibilities. And off she would go, carrying a bundle of stuff. I knew she would be back in about an hour or so, so I took the opportunity to get comfy, and have a rest on my bed. An hour had gone by, and then two hours. By this time, I was starting to feel the need for the loo, and I mean a number two! I was still quite chilled, as I was pretty sure she would be back very shortly, and the first thing she would do would be to take me to the fields. But no, 20 minutes on, and there was still no sign of her. At this point I was really starting to get a bit stressed as I really needed a poo. I tried pacing around the room to distract myself but that didn't help in fact that made me need to go more. I sat down. Thinking the urge would go. It did not. For the love of dogs, what was I to do! I was actually starting to feel a little cross, how could this be happening to me? I whined a little, but no one could hear as they were all probably at that meeting. Arghhhhh. This was going to be a disaster; I was definitely regretting the treats I had been given earlier. Oh, I wished I had resisted the temptation, but it's so hard, when its something so delicious looking. It would have been rude not to.

And then it happened, on the brand-new carpet. I could no longer contain what was now bursting to come out. I was frantically pawing around the room, to find a hidey place, but nowhere, and I certainly wasn't going to do it by my bedding. So, I did what any other fraught dog would do, I went to the middle of the room, squatted down and unleashed hell. The relief was unbelievable. It was over in the blink of an eye. I really could not have held it in for another millisecond. However, it was quite possibly the nastiest, stinkiest pile of mess I had ever done in my life. I can't begin to tell you what the smell was like. Oh, how I wished I could open the window! Furthermore, typical, just minutes after the deed had landed, a man came in to get a pen. I tell you what I have never seen a person turn green, nor move so fast to the door to get out. Naturally, I was mortified. And I just slunk my way over to my bed. I couldn't even blame one of the spaniels, because how on earth would they have got in, in the first place with the door closed! With the man gone, I knew in my bones, Mum would be here any moment. Sure enough, I didn't have to wait long for Mum to arrive. My head was down, and I was trying to be as small as possible. I just wanted the ground to swallow me up. She let out a really strange noise, like coughing. Her tone of voice definitely indicated surprise, as opposed to anger. Then to my disbelief, she knelt down by me and held my head up and gave me hug. But not for long, as then with great purpose, holding her arm across her nose and mouth, she strode across the room and flung open the windows. I think we both gasped in the fresh air. Then poor Mum left the room and was soon back with bottles of stuff and lots of paper. I really couldn't make eye contact as she scraped up my mountainous mess on her hands and knees and scrubbed the once pristine carpet. It was at this point that the big boss man, poked his head in. I could sense Mum was anxious, but all I heard was a bellow of laughter from him, and the sigh of relief from Mum. I think it was about three days before we could return to our office. I'm so thankful she didn't shout at me; it truly was the most awful embarrassing event of my life. That's why I love her so much, she just knows I'd never have done something like this if I had not been in such a hopeless situation. Unconditional love is a wonderful thing.

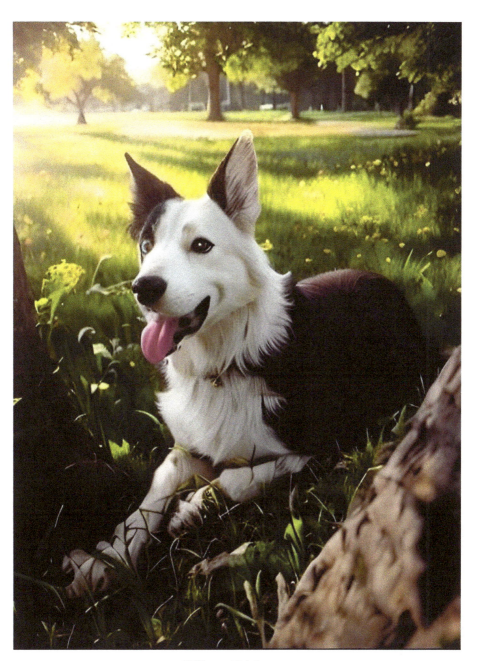

Chilling at Wakehurst

CHAPTER 10 THE GREAT ROAD TRIP

I can't possibly begin to tell you about this adventure without introducing you to my best pal, Snowy. And strange as my doggie friends may think, Snowy was a cat. And even stranger a black cat. For this story I need to go back a little.

We were living in Ardingly, and one of Mum's friends from the Bothe at Wakehurst had a new job working with and looking after a lot of cats. One day Mum decided to go and visit her at her workplace, and of course, she took me along. I was expecting to go inside, but Mum thought it was best I wait in the car. So, there I stayed, sat up straight with an unwavering eye on the door she had gone through. A short while later she came back, and I could detect her happy vibes. She was talking to me a lot on the way home. I wondered what was going on. I was naturally curious, and as we drove, I mulled over the likelihoods.

We went back a few times, and one occasion, Mum took my blanket, which I thought was a bit bizarre. Again, I remained in the car. Watching her walk in, with my blanket. When she reappeared, she had a different blanket. I knew that because it had a completely different smell, and not one I recognised, and when we got home, she put that blanket in my bed, for me to sleep with. It didn't smell too bad actually. It was definitely an animal smell, but not dog. Hmm, the plot had thickened.

On our final visit to this mystery place, when Mum came in to view, she had a box in her arms. I was in the boot part of the car, she popped the box down on the ground and opened the back doors, and very gently lifted and placed the box on the back seat. Then I heard a shifty sort of shuffle noise. And what's more there was a very familiar smell.... Hang on THE BLANKET. I could smell the blanket. The penny dropped, there was an animal in the box! Mum was bringing home a friend for me. Yeah! I was so excited, I love presents, as you all know and the whole way home peering over the seat, I fixated my eyes on that box. All the way home Mum didn't stop talking, in that kind reassuring voice that she has.

Once we pulled up at home, rather than letting me out straight away, Mum carefully cradled the box and took it inside, and left me in the boot. By now I was mad with excitement. Yes, I confess I may have even whined. I just wanted to be released from the boot and dive into that box! Then when what seemed like an eternity, Mum came and got me. But we didn't go through the front door instead she walked me round the back, to the patio doors. And then that's when I had my first glance at what had come home. A CAT!!! A black cat in my lounge! Wow, my friends were never going to believe this. I was unable to contain myself a second longer, and to get this cats attention I started to leap up against the windows, pretty much, 'hey cat, I'm here' type of thing. But cat didn't seem interested in the slightest, it just sat there with its back to me. What kind of manners is that I thought. Rude. Typical cat behaviour.

I still had my lead on, when Mum cautiously slid the door open. And in we went. Very slowly Mum and I approached cat. Cat by now was watching me intently, and when we were close enough to each other we had a good old mutual sniff. Yep, definitely that blanket smell. And cat didn't seem disturbed by my smell either. It was at this point that Mum unclipped my lead. Yeah, now I could get really close to investigate. Perfect. The blooming thing only went and swiped at me, which sent me running from the lounge, with cat in full pursuit. Leaving me no option but to pelt it up the stairs. Cat just sat at the bottom for a bit, in a 'you shalt not pass' sort of way. Rather smug if I'm honest. I tried to act natural, regain my dignity, and settled down at the top of the stairs, like this was what I would normally do. A bit awkward. Ultimately this was my house, I was Mum's favourite and cat was going to have to get used to me. In due course, Cat sauntered off to the lounge, and Mum from the bottom of the stairs coaxed me back down, which after some time I did in a gingerly manner.

And so, this edginess went on for a few weeks, until gradually Cat – who I came to know as Snowy, began to offer the paw of friendship. She would kiss me good morning, and I would reciprocate with a big lick. Snowy was so tiny, that I would literally cover her face. Not sure she was too keen on that, but she appreciated the sentiment, I'm sure. She even began to get playful, and would run up to me to take a swipe, then run off and I would chase her around the house, until she would lightly spring up out of reach onto a piece of furniture. Intelligent move. I loved playing those games with her.

Right, now you have been formally introduced to my friend Snowy, lets get back to the adventure. I think I was about five years old. The world had gone peculiar. When Mum and I went for our long walks, there was no one to be seen, and hardly any cars. When we crossed the odd dog, I noticed on the humans, they had mouth coverings. We didn't even go to the cafes anymore. It was during this ghostly time, that Mum began putting lots of things in boxes, until one morning, she filled her car with bags, put Snowy and I in the car (Snowy in her travel cage) and started up the engine. We were going on a journey to the unknown. And what a long trip it was! Days.

We had lots of stops though for pee breaks and little walks. I got to watch all the cars whizzing by from the window, that thing I have loved since I was a pup. The lorries were the best, and as they passed, I would salute them with a bark. Probably annoyed Snowy a bit. And when it got dark, we stopped at these big houses with lots of people living in them. We didn't really socialise with the humans. Though some seemed friendly enough. Some were grumpy too. We didn't have a kitchen or lounge or anything. Just a big bedroom. Some were rather nice. Snowy spent ages sniffing everywhere.

And we got to explore outside. Even Snowy had a collar and lead and came for walks. We must have looked a right pair. Ha.

At long last we rolled up at our destination. A rustic little house with a sea view. It had a farm-like feel to it, though without the animals. I could barely contain myself, I love the beach, and I could smell, hear and taste the sea. And there was so much room for me to explore and run around right on the doorstep. Not like the towns we had lived in. And so peaceful. Mum was going back and forth from the car, taking out those bags and while she was busy with that, I had a wee in the new garden. This was after all going to be my new home. We were in Scotland on the Isle of Lewis.

Me and my best friend Snowy

CHAPTER 11 ISLAND LIFE

Our first night in the croft was freezing! At this point, there was no heating. But we all kept warm by cuddling up to each other. I didn't have to wait long before of some of Mum's friends and family came to visit, and they helped her fix up the croft. I can't begin to tell you what a stunning view we had. I mean we were literally right on a beach. It was a paradise. It felt so free. We could do anything we liked. It was here I had some of my most incredible walks. Even Snowy would sometimes tag along on those long beach walks. I probably saw some of the most beautiful sandy beaches ever while we lived up there. The coast was rugged, great for honing in my rock-climbing skills. And there was wildlife I had never seen. Animals like seals.

These large greyish animals, with their massive soppy eyes, their bodies round in the middle and narrow at the ends, a bit like a rugby ball, were fun to swim with. Their diving skills were like none I had ever seen. Literally one minute one would be bobbing by me, the next it had simply vanished. And they sometimes stayed under forever. Far longer than I ever could. I used to challenge myself with a fun little game I came up with, guess where the seal would pop up. Some were timid and would stay back watching at a distance, but some were more spirited and playful. They made strange noises too, when they chatted. Under water it was a sort of click click sound. But on the surface, like a bark! Sometimes I was sure they were trying to tell me something and in some odd way they reminded me a bit of dogs.

There was one time, Mum and I were having one of our wonderful shoreline strolls by the croft. In the near distance I could see what I thought at first was a dog, washed up. I was seriously concerned thinking the worse and I raced over to it. It startled me when it hissed at me. Fierce for a little thing. Well, at least it was alive. Phew. It was in fact a baby seal. It must have got separated from its mum. I can't imagine anything worse. Poor little thing. I probably came across as bit scary, with all my fur, and I realised I couldn't just abandon it. I therefore made the decision to sit at its foot. Mum was already talking to someone on her phone at this point. Then some people arrived. But they didn't come down, they kept at a distance, watching us. I stayed put, I wasn't going to let anything happen to this little'un. Over time the sea was getting closer and closer. Each wave lapping nearer and nearer to my ward. Until eventually, the seal had the sea at its feet. Once that happened, he was able to crawl his way in a bit deeper, and then just like that was gone. Like it had never happened. I got lots of pats and strokes that day.

And there were other animals that were to come into our lives. Mum only went and got BIRDS!! Chickens actually. They were feisty little friends and chasing them was out of the question. Even Snowy, who definitely had her eyes on them as a potential food source, left them alone. And so a friendship based on mutual respect grew. They all had vaccine names, Moderna, Pfizer, Seneca, and Astra.

Moderna was the one I really connected with, and even Snowy felt that special bond. She was a right mother hen, and often we would all snuggle together on the sofa. Then there was Pfizer. Probably the naughtiest and funniest. You know I actually think she thought I was a horse or something, as she liked nothing better than to jump on my back. I also had responsibilities with the girls. Using my in-built herding talent, I was charged with rounding them up at the end of the day, making sure they were all safe in their little house. Sometimes it was a bit of a nightmare, as possibly they thought it was a game, but they would flap and leap up, often over me! But I always got the job done. We even got a couple of ducks. Actually, eight to be precise. What a funny sound they make. They too were on my job list to make sure they were tucked in at night too. Sadly, I recall an incident, where we (myself Snowy and Mum) were all sleeping. It was the dead of night. When suddenly I heard a noise coming from the ducks. Mum was sound asleep. Snowy had heard it too, and she began to swipe at Mum's face. I was barking, wake up wake up. Mum did wake up, and she even went to the window to see if anything untoward was going on. But she came back to bed. Cuddled us and went back to sleep. I definitely had a sense of foreboding and I knew Snowy was feeling it too. Well, the next morning, when we went to open the duck house, only seven waddled out. The only evidence of kidnap, some smallish paw prints, not a fox, it didn't smell like a fox. Possibly an otter. I should have been there for that duck. It's a regret of mine. Mum also got some little yellow birds, that had the prettiest songs to sing. And they lived inside. Thankfully for them, they were in a house with little bars. I think if Snowy could, she would have had them for breakfast! We had become an extended happy family.

We stayed there for nearly a year having the best and wildest times, then Mum decided we should go back South. The journey home was a tight squeeze, and we had the yellow birds with us too. I remember Mum would put the music on in the car, and they loved it, tweeting away. Again, we took our time going back home, and stayed in various places. I remember the wooden barrel thing. That was my favourite. And the others apart from Mum loved that place too. When we finally arrived back, we didn't have our old house anymore and so we went to grandad Dels for a bit. We needed to find a new place to live. Of course, I helped Mum house hunting, and eventually, I found one for her, marked my territory and the house was ours.

This next part of my life is one that fills me with great sadness. We were still living with grandad Del, when I noticed Snowy was not her usual self. She was getting on a bit, probably nearly ten years older than me. Mum kept taking her to the cat doctor, and bringing her home. I did my bit nursing, cuddling up to her, gently nudging her and giving her licks. But she didn't get better, and one day she went off in the car with Mum and she never came home. I was confused, bereft, and even angry at Mum. She would try and hold me for comfort, and I would pull away. I could still smell Snowy everywhere. But she was gone. Mum was of course sad too. It was a really difficult time for me. My best friend, my sister from another mother, the one I shared such a great Scottish adventure with, we were double trouble and she was now never going to walk through the door again. I have to admit the yellow bird was a great comfort at this tragic time (there was only one as one had passed on – Mum showed it to me, and I was able to kiss it goodbye, which meant a lot to me). We talked a lot about Snowy, and through that came peace and acceptance. Time is a great healer

Me, Snowy, Mum & Pfizer the naughty Hen

Me and the seal pup at the Isle of Lewis

CHAPTER 12 HAPPY WOOF WOOF TO ME

I have come to learn there is a very special day once a year, where I am celebrated more than ever. I get to do whatever I like, am given presents and treats galore, and people come to see me. It's a time of year, when hot days have passed and are replaced with cooler air, but not so cold as to shiver. I know when that day has arrived every year, as the day begins with a very special breakfast for me, made by Mum who as she carries in the tray of eggs, bacon, toast and a sausage, is singing. And the day gets better and better. After breakfast I charge downstairs, and there on the sofa is a big roundish ball, on a piece of string, floating in the air above my presents. I have to confess I can barely contain myself. I love pressies. I wait eagerly for Mum, who grabs another cup of tea, and we then sit together. Let the opening begin. Now you might think just because I'm a dog, that Mum has to open the gifts for me. You would be wrong, as I am very skilled at gently pulling off the paper all by myself. I remember my first special day, and getting so many yummy treats. More than I had ever seen at one time in my life. As I could do what I liked, I ate them all in one day! Well, I felt it the next day let me tell you. I had the maddest zoomies ever. I was so hyper, I didn't know my own strength, and for reasons that I can't explain, I moved Mum's sofa across the room with my head and then had a gnawing frenzy on the bottom of the bannister. Ooops.

I digress. After presents, Mum takes me on my much-loved long walk, and the floaty thing is attached to me so it follows me everywhere. I am the talk of the park, all the other dogs stare in wonder and their mums and dads stop and smile and say things to me. Mum seems so happy. When we arrive home, the postman has been and so I watch Mum opening my cards and putting them up for all to see. It seems I'm a popular boy. Then we get dressed for a posh lunch. Sometimes I wear a hat, sometimes a bow tie, one time Mum even put a very sparkling stringy things around my ankles. It really showed off my slim ankles very nicely. For lunch, I have steak, and my favourite pudding, ice cream. It's heavenly. You might think that's it, but no, back home my dog friends come over for cake! My favourite Boneo and Dog Chocolate. It really is such a wonderful day. I am so spoilt, and blessed to have such wonderful friends and a thoughtful Mum.

My 10th Birthday. I still look good for my age, dont you know!

CHAPTER 13 A DOG IS NOT JUST FOR CHRISTMAS

There is one other time of year where there are presents to open. It's usually the coldest time of year and Mum puts a tree up in the home. She beautifies it with lots of shiny ball things. I even have my own decoration, a little boy with a very long nose, made of wood, she says I'm her Pinocchio and if we wish hard enough I may become a real boy. With my paw I show Mum where to hang it on the tree. I tell you what, that tree really makes the room smell nice. Sends my nose into overdrive. It's a time of year, where I dress up too. Sometimes I go glam, in gold and sequins, other times, like an elf, or I wear a rather dashing red coat with white fur trimming and a black belt. Other times it's plain old embarrassing, especially when I had a white-bearded man, with a big hat, tied on my back. But it makes Mum laugh though, so I go with the flow and get into the spirit. Sometimes Mum and I co-ordinate and wear the same outfits.

On this day every year, it also begins with a really special breakfast, in bed of course. Salmon don't you know. And a poached egg. Then she gives me this giant sock, which had been hanging off the bottom of the bed which is full to the brim with goodies. I get so excited, and together we take turns unwrapping. There is music on too, lots of jingly songs, and of course Mum is singing away. It's very jolly. But there is more, when we go downstairs under the tree are even more gifts! But Mum makes me wait. I pretend to not notice this exciting pile, and when she isn't looking, I have tried to sneak one open. One time, I found a knitted scarf in the paper, and Mum had to re-wrap it as it was for Grandad Del. Ooops.

Talking of him, every year he takes me for a walk to see the houses garnished to the hilt in lights, it's dazzling. As good as watching car headlights even. Lunch is a mouth-watering serving of meat, roast potatoes, sausages wrapped in bacon, veg and lashings of gravy. To die for. On and off in the day we open more presents, I know when it's my turn as Mum smiles at me and says the magic words 'present Monty'. And then with our bellies full and ready to explode there is a big walk. In the park I see my friends, and we show each other our new clothes or toys. It's very cool, and a joyous atmosphere. When we get home, back in the warmth, we curl up together and watch some TV, I love the film The Incredible Journey. Do you know when I was younger, seeing dogs on the box would throw me. I actually thought they were real and I would go behind the TV to seek them out. Took me quite a while to realise they weren't really there.

Yes, this day is marvellous, presents, friends, family, dancing, great food and favourite films. Simply perfect.

Me standing in for Rudolph

CHAPTER 14 FOR THE LOVE OF WOODS & SQUIRRELS

I was just a teenager when Ursula burst into my world. Now I have mentioned previously I used to go to work with Mum, but there were some days when she would go solo and I would stay to look after the home. I was first alerted to the arrival of Ursula by an incredibly loud ear-splitting voice. In all honesty, I am not keen on deafening noise, but tell me a dog who is. Having said that she did grab my attention, and I was curious about her. Once she settled down, I padded over to her to have a good sniff. It was quite a confusing smell as I could smell a lot of different types of dogs on her. But hey, anyone who smells of dog is a potential friend of mine.

We then went outside the house, and she had a van. It looked rather special. I had my lead on, and as we approached the door, Mum knelt down and gave me a big hug and said I was to be a good boy. The door was opened and inside were other dogs. All sat there staring at me. In I jumped. They all seemed to know each other, and the mood was friendly and jolly. They seemed like they would be good company. Ursula climbed into the front, and started up the engine. Ooooh, we were going on a drive. I just hoped I was coming back. Mum stood, one arm wrapped around her waist and the other waving at me. I watched her intently, as she grew smaller and smaller in the distance.

Soon, I could feel we were on a steep winding climb. All of us sat there swaying from side to side as Ursula navigated the sharp bends. The other dogs were getting quite excited, like they knew something good was coming. Out of the window I could see open grassland, and sheep. We must have been quite high as I had that weird sensation of pressure in my ears, then heard a pop from them. After a short time, we pulled into a car park and off went the engine. The other dog's excitement was beginning to rub off on me, and I was as keen as they were to leap out of the van.

We then left the car park, still on our leads. Some of the dogs were pulling, so I had a little quiet word with them, 'We won't get there any quicker (wherever there is) and you'll get a sore neck'. Once on a path, our leads were taken off. Now I've seen greyhounds run, and they are fast. But these dogs scattered at speed in all directions. Some zig-zagging nose to the ground and some darting ahead. Ursula didn't seem worried, but it's then that understood why I was here. To help her keep them in line. Like I had seen my mum and dad herding, I was to be her personal shepherd. A very important job. I was a natural, and we walked for miles and miles, me now and again reminding my new friends to stay together. We went through small dense woody bits, open fields that sent my nose senses in to overdrive, probably all the flowers up there. And I had never seen so many butterflies, flitting about. It was marvellous. After what seemed like hours and probably was, Ursula took me back home to Mum. I was so overjoyed to see her, bouncing up on her, desperate to tell her about my amazing day. I was tired too, as we had walked for miles. I woofed goodbye to my new charges, still sat in the van and gave Ursula a thank you lick. I wondered how I had done in my new role as her shepherd?

Well, I must have done ok. As I was collected again, and again and again. And each time was an awesome adventure. Obviously, I had my duties, lending a paw to Ursula managing the others. But by now we were all such great pals, a tight knit pack and they knew the modus operandi. Don't run off. The places I visited were absolutely fantastic. I loved the forest, where I would let my fur down a little and chase the birds and the squirrels. As stealthy as I could be, I could NEVER catch the birds, apart from one odd incident, when through the trees I clocked a flapper on the ground. Hey hey, potential to grab one. I hurtled forward, reached the bird, who instead of flying off in mad panic, like I expected, just sat there looking at me. I was so unprepared for this, as like I say I have never actually caught a bird. Its beady eyes fixed on me, unwavering, daring me. A little unnerving. So, what did I do? Nothing. Put my nose to the ground and trotted off like nothing had happened. I hope the other dogs hadn't seen me so confused. But that's when I understood what I liked about birds. Not the catch, but the chase.

I have such happy memories of my time spent with Ursula. And when we moved, I was sad those days had come to an end. I had even got used to her animated and energetic voice. We had formed such a close friendship and I really missed her company, and the other dogs. But on a plus, Mum and her have remained friends, and Ursula does come to visit us. And when she does, it's like I just saw her the other day. We just pick up. I think that's the sign of a good friends' thing. You know when you don't see each other for yonks, but when you do, it's like you were never apart.

Squirrels!!!!!

CHAPTER 15 GOING VEGGIE

I felt awful. What was wrong with me? I was always so exhausted. Could it be my age? I was getting on a bit now, nearly ten. I couldn't even bring myself to chase my beloved ball. Even when we were in the woods and I'd spot a squirrel, I felt too lethargic to chase. And my coat which was typically shiny and gorgeous, was looking flat and dull. Something was off. I was clearly not my usual bouncy self and Mum had noticed and took me to see the dog doctor. When he put me on the table, seriously I could have just curled up and gone to sleep. The doctor didn't do very much, he just looked at my eyes, ran his hands over me, Mum and him were chatting and I just wanted to go home, to my bedroom. My prayers were answered and we were soon back in the car going home.

Some time passed and Mum took me back to dog doctor. This time he poked me with a sharp thing, it had a tube on it, and started to fill with crimson. I think that's my blood! Then back home. Then back again the next day! This time, they took a little bit of fur away with a buzzy thing and the doctor had a weird thing in his hand it looked a bit like dog bone, which he then began to roll around on my skin. It felt cold and a bit slimy, and while this was happening him and Mum were looking at a TV in the room. It didn't take long, and then it was back home.

Oh my dog, my next meal was meatless. WHAT?! Within a short space of time, I was eating only vegetables—I mean, exclusively vegetables. A bit of a shocker to begin with. I'm a dog after all. I mean I've had vegetables before, especially when I have gone out with nan and Mum for a Sunday roast. And I have always liked carrots and eating those green things that look like mini trees. All lathered in gravy. But now, my roasts had become chickenless! But the remarkable thing was I was starting to feel more alive. My energy was coming back, and I was excited again when Mum threw the ball. Chasing it down, bringing it back to be tossed again. I was even jumping through the hoop again. Definitely, I had got my mojo back. I was introduced to so many new delicious flavours. There were these dried orangey things, that looked a bit like ginger cat ears, and they were so sweet. When Mum and I would sit on the sofa, watching TV she would put on a tasty spread wedged between us on a wooden board. And then there were new weekend breakfast goodies such as an egg which Mum would bring up on a tray to bed. A perfect way to start a day. In the week I now had a small block of something wheaty that starts off light and crispy, then Mum would add some water, and it would transform into a beigy mush. Not a bad flavour and it would set me up, giving me loads of oomph to tackle the day.

I definitely began to feel a lot better. We returned to the dog doctor after a few months of adjusting to this new way of life. I could tell from the way they spoke that him and Mum are very pleased, and Mum smiled loads. For my part, I felt 10 years younger and my joie de vivre has been restored.

Not that there haven't been times when I craved meat. Situations, such as when my dog pals have come to stay. They would get raw meat for lunch and tea! In these circumstances I would prepare mentally and repeat my mantra over and over 'Monty keep away from the raw'. Naturally Mum would be really considerate and mealtimes set them up in a different room to have their food so I wouldn't have to use every bone of willpower to not dive in nor look longingly at their bowls, which would have possibly made my guests feel uncomfortable. As time has gone on the temptation has become less and my craving and love of meat has diminished. Even at the garden centre where they always had meaty dog snacks available and still do, I am able to walk by without even drooling.

I'm discovering new cuisine too. Like the other day for instance, Mum and I had these little yellowy plump things in black shells. They tasted a little like the sea and were divine; tender yet a little chewy. It took me back to my island days. Happy times.

Finally, I'm sleeping better, which no doubt is helping me feel more alive in the daytime. Before bed, Mum gives me a magic drink. It has gentle notes of apple, with a mellow honey-like sweetness, and from the first sip it feels wonderfully soothing. After that, I feel calm and sleepy.

PAWS FOR THOUGHT

There's more life in the 'old' dog yet.

How could I possibly eat you anyway!

CHAPTER 16 WHAT THEY SAY

"Dual eyed with the brain of a scientist and can creep up on pigeons with the stealth of a cat". Mark

"Monty has an amazing spirit & a beautiful personality. He cares so much for his friends and family that it's hardly believable he's actually a dog. When he was asked to go & find Snowy, he would nip off & bring her back. He was so gentle with his chicken & duck family that there was never a moment of worry how he would behave".

"Monty was one of my first fur clients when I started my dog care business & it was always a challenge to tire him out, but I did it at least once! So many people know Monty by his stunning looks & it is a joy to see him enjoy the love he gets from people". Ursula Xx

"A funny loyal intelligent pooch that once pooped in my office". Peter

"Monty is one of a kind. He's been a shining star when you needed the light the most, and for that, Monty will always be extra special". Silvia Xxxxxx

"Whenever you see him, You just have to smile. Hes like if the sun became a dog. Like you see him and all your worries fade away. You can't be sad in his presence". Lana xx

"Monty is a lovely, loyal dog. He's been with Mum through the roughest times and is (and always will be) her best friend". Glyn

"They say you can't teach an old dog New Tricks, that I can't believe! Monty has taught me a lot; he knows how to get inside your head with his wonderful mannerisms which is a great to watch. He has charisma and charm far superior than most humans; they say a dog is a man's best friend. Not quite true, he is Mum's best friend and the bond between them is so special. Monty knows how to manipulate you with expressions which are joy to see. To watch him play and dance with Mum is Magic so you see, he belongs to be in volumes not just a book". Delboy X

"Monty came into my life when he became my granddaughter's adorable puppy. He quickly became just like a naughty child, loveable & cheeky. His ears lopsided, one always up & the other down. His eyes add to his charm, one blue-white, the other brown. He loves all sorts of outings and loves his journeys in cars if he can catch a lift. Monty loves swimming in the sea, especially in the Isle of Lewis with the seals around him and can run faster than a greyhound after his beloved ball". Joyce x

Side-by-side every sunset and sunrise

Milton Keynes UK
Ingram Content Group UK Ltd.
UKHW050221280324
440095UK00001B/2